The
Baby Boomer
Millennial
DIVIDE

Making it Work
At Work

The Baby Boomer Millennial *DIVIDE*

Making it Work At Work

Beverly Mahone
with Chris Gure

DocUmeant *Publishing*
244 5th Avenue
Suite G-200
NY, NY 10001
646-233-4366
www.DocUmeantPublishing.com

Published by
DocUmeant Publishing
244 5th Avenue, Suite G-200
NY, NY 10001

646-233-4366

Library of Congress Control Number: 2016961041

ISBN 13: 978-1-9378-0179-3

Contents

Acknowledgments vii

Foreword. xi

The Baby Boomer Perspective 1

PART I: PASSING THE BATON FROM BABY
 BOOMERS TO MILLENNIALS. 3

Changing of the Guard 5
 Who are the Millennials? 9
 Millennial Attitudes Toward
  Baby Boomers 15
  So, What do Millennials Think About
   Boomers in the Workplace? 17

Do's and Don'ts for Baby Boomers in
 the Workplace 21
 Don't. 22
 Do. 23

Discrimination Against Boomers in the
 Workplace *(my personal commentary)*. . . .27
Keys to Working Together Successfully 31

Who is Beverly Mahone 35

Resources. 37

The Millennial Perspective 39

PART II: ACCEPTING THE BATON FROM BABY
  BOOMERS TO MILLENNIALS 41

Changing of the Guard 43

  Who are the Baby Boomers? 47

  Millennials Meeting Boomers at Work 51

  How Baby Boomers View Millennials 53
    *Their Number One Complaint: We are
    Obsessed with Technology* 53

    *Millennials Have Earned the Reputation as the
    "Job-Hopping" Generation.* 54

    Some Believe We Crave Recognition 54

    We Don't Take Criticism Well 54

    *Millennials Are Not Loyal to Their
    Employers* 55

  Understanding Boomers in the Workplace . . 57

Who is Chris Gure? 63

Acknowledgments

This guide would be nothing without the input of my millennial friend, Chris Gure. We met a few years ago during the beginning stages of his career as a financial planner and I am excited to see where life is taking him. What I love about this young man is if he believes in something he goes all in and he gives me hope for his generation.

This guide is also dedicated the many wonderful Millennials I have come in contact with over the past several years: Karkeshia Hart, Nicole Fitts, Danita Smallwood, Erica Bellamy, Travis Perry, Trey Blue, Chloe, Dejuan Burgess, Laquwna Daniels, Tykisha Leach, Whitney Del Rosario, and Tajon Mitchel. Interacting with them makes me laugh a lot and sometimes leaves me shaking my head (hashtag #smh in their language). They have inspired me in ways they will never know or, perhaps, appreciate. They are my "adopted" young adult children.

Speaking of children, a special shout-out to my daughter Janie, who has grown up to be the spitting image of me in some ways but many of her actions are reminders that we are light years apart and sometimes it's best for me to stay in my lane.

A great big shout out to J&S Photography in Durham, NC (Jen and Steve), who were responsible for the photo on the book cover. They put up with my drama and numerous schedule changes and still managed to create magic with the camera lens. I highly recommend them. (jandsphoto.net)

Speaking of the photo shoot, a big ups to Kirstie Jenkins, who stepped in at the last minute and agreed to be a part of the book. Although we hadn't seen each other in over a year, she was still the same bubbly young lady I remember when we worked together. Her personality and, especially her laugh, is infectious and I am honored that she allows me to be a part of her Millennial world.

A huge thank you goes to Brianca Trent and Kymberlee Holloway who didn't hesitate when I asked them for their input on this guide. All I can say is, *"Be careful for you ask for."* You'll see what I mean later in this guide. #noshade

I was inspired in many ways by several fellow baby boomers. Angela Fisher, Leland Brame and I met in a training class and immediately bonded. Of course, age had a lot to do with it but we also got to share life experiences and "remember when" stories. I'm not sure how I would've survived training had they not been there because, trust me, being surrounded by Millennials all day, every day can be mentally draining, especially in a Call Center environment.

All I can say about Cynthia White is thank God for her! She has prayed with and for me and even when I went into deep isolation, she kept the lifeline out for me to grab on to when I was ready. And she always gives me feedback straight with no chaser.

Who better to write the Introduction of this book than my friend Olalah Njenga. Not only is she a business owner who has managed the different generations in her Company, but she also calls herself "a proud mother of two well-adjusted Millennials." She is truly a business guru and my go-to person when it comes to Marketing.

This is the third book Ginger Marks of DocUmeant Publishing and I have worked on together. She always goes above and beyond what is asked of her to make sure the finished product is better than great!

My husband Nate is my sounding board and the only one who can reel me back in when I've gone too far. He keeps me grounded and no matter how many re-writes he is *forced* to listen to, he always says *"That's good!"*

And finally, a special thank you to and for my grandson Jarod Lewis Bryant. He is the light of my life and if I live long enough I'll be writing about his "Z" generation.

Foreword

Over the years of running my company, I have hired, fired, managed and lead many employees. Some have made me a better leader, while others have made me question my own sanity. I was building a business while raising two children and that armed me with a unique ability to know when to sit back and watch things play out, as opposed to always jumping into the mix.

As the dynamic of the world has morphed, so has the workplace. There was once a time when my employees and I were relatively in the same generation so we could swap stories, tell off-color jokes and make references to the past with a nostalgic sigh. But those days are gone. Long Gone. Today, the average workplace, including my own, is a hurried, always connected to some device, break-neck speed, coffee-induced microcosm of twenty-somethings, thirty-somethings, forty-somethings and fifty-somethings all vying for one thing—relevance.

For many managers, the modern workplace is one part opportunity, one part overwhelm. On any given day we are excited about finding interesting ways to capitalize on the exceptional combined talents of our employees, while we are stretched to figure out how to adjust our style of management to be able to treat each employee like an individual. This constant shifting between opportunity and overwhelm is not only necessary, but it's non-negotiable as a manager.

While Millennials certainly get credit for being the most vocal about doing meaningful work . . . relevant work . . . work that inspires them, excites them and challenges them, they are not alone in having this desire. Feeling like you are making a difference, contributing to something bigger than yourself and having an impact are also part of the workplace goals that many forty-somethings and fifty-somethings have as well. But for twenty-somethings and thirty-somethings, these are absolutes. They live, work and play by these concepts daily. If we manage them, then we are responsible for creating a workplace where they can make a difference, contribute to something bigger and have an impact. For if we don't create a workplace where Millennials can be relevant, they will surely find another place to work where they can do just that.

If we take nothing else from the social experiment that we call "working across the generations", it should be this . . . Millennials want to be mentored, guided, coached, steered, praised, recognized, promoted, engaged, inspired, heard, and lead. But they do not want to be managed.

If you find yourself supervising Millennials, take some advice from a business owner who has raised two Millennials (I have the premature gray hair to prove it) and sent them both into the world to make a difference, contribute to something bigger and have an impact. Find clever ways to camouflage the need to manage Millennials, just like those cool moms who know how to hide vegetables inside of home-made muffins.

Why this *Baby Boomer/Millennial Guide to Understanding Each Other in the Workplace* is important right now:

Managers and employees alike need a field manual of sorts to navigate this new terrain—this new workplace where twenty-somethings and fifty-somethings work alongside one another. We need a guide to help us translate our respective generational norms into a universal language where we can live, work and sometimes play together without feeling misunderstood and dismissed. Today's modern workplace can be a battlefield of crossed wires and hurt feelings when someone who is twenty years your junior or senior makes a play for your pet project and threatens to steal your thunder. How do we find common ground and collaboration when we feel dissed and blindsided? Ask the expert, Bev Mahone.

Bev is a "grandma who gets it". I look to Bev's irreverent musings and insightful nuggets about all things boomer/millennial related because she is one of the savviest boomers I know. Thank goodness Bev has taken up the mantle of helping business professionals across the generations navigate the new workplace dynamic. Without her wisdom and expertise, those of us who manage and lead across the generations would be lost. Bev is a generational tour guide for the workplace. We crave her know-how to keep from banging our heads on the wall. Bev's approach is not for the faint of heart. She tells it like it is because she has lived it—and still does! If you want an expert's perspective about how to survive the boomer/millennial battlefield, ask Bev. Not only does she get it, but she wrote the book on it.

Olalah Njenga
CEO, YellowWood Group
Proud mother of two well-adjusted Millennials
www.yellowwoodgroup.com

The Baby Boomer Perspective

PART I

*Passing the Baton from
Baby Boomers to Millennials*

"Change is the law of life and those who only look to the past or to the present are certain to miss the future."

~John F. Kennedy

Changing of the Guard

Hello my dear know-it-all, *been-there-done-that* fellow baby boomers:

In case you didn't get the memo, a changing of the guard is taking place. Members of our generation are slowly being pushed aside for the dawning of a new era. The Age of Aquarius is over. Disco died a long time ago and Hip-Hop rules the music world. The *suits* in the workplace have been replaced with polos and jeans. The art of excellent face-to-face communication skills have been taken over by voiceless texting and the deceptive images made possible by new online technology platforms.

The Millennial Generation has arrived and taken over America by storm. According to statistics released by the U.S. Census Bureau in June 2015, "Millennials, or America's youth born between 1982 and 2000, now number 83.1 million and represent more than one quarter of the nation's population. Their size exceeds that of the 75.4 million baby boomers."[1]

1 Born between 1946–1964

As it relates to the workforce, more than one-in-three American workers today are Millennials, surpassing baby boomers in 2014. By 2025, it is estimated they will make up 75 percent of the workforce. These youngsters have entered the workforce with new attitudes and perspectives on what their employment should be like and how relationships between employers and employees should be developed.

They are not interested in hierarchy or the "kiss ass" mentality to get ahead on the job. Former MTV Executive Nick Shore said "Millennials find hierarchies difficult to understand because they didn't grow up with it. An ideocracy should reign in the workplace, most Millennials believe, in which everyone should be heard from and the best ideas win out, regardless of who has been on the job longer, or who has a corner office."[2]

Unlike us, if they're not happy with the way things are going, they'll just look for something else. We, meanwhile, suck it up and continue to work and complain until we're fired or retirement comes.

So, why is a guide like this necessary? It is important because as long as you and I remain in the job market, we are more than likely going to be working side by side with millennials. We are going to be challenged daily by the way they say and do things. We will cringe over their lack of conformity and their snub of the established "it's always been done this way" rules.

---

2 Source: http://business.time.com/2012/03/29/
millennials-vs-baby-boomers-who-would-you-rather-hire/

This guide is especially relevant if you are a baby boomer in a supervisory/managerial position because you will be responsible for trying to get the best out of them while encouraging them to appreciate working for you and the Company you represent.

"Parents who complain about the younger generation are really just saying that their generation did a crappy job raising their kids."

~Author unknown

WHO ARE THE MILLENNIALS?

"They are the first generation to have computers in the home and in the classroom, to have always had a cell phone, music downloads, instant messaging and hundreds of cable channels." [3]

How ironic that the creative and technical minds of baby boomers like Steve Jobs and Bill Gates would lead to the technology boom fueled by the Millennial Generation. It's all about Snapchat, Google Hangout, YouTube, Skype and Smartphones. They would rather send a text in seconds rather than communicate in person. I don't know about you but there is nothing more annoying to me than to try to have a conversation with a young person while they are deeply engaged in their phones.

According the Pew Research Center, Millennials are described as "confident, self-expressive, liberal, upbeat, and open to change." They are also multi-taskers, achievement-oriented, less religious and less likely to have served in the military.

---

3 Source: Boomers to Millennials: Generational Attitudes article by Cara Newman

In order to work effectively with them, we should take some time to understand who makes up the Millennial Generation. First and foremost, they were raised by protective parents (you may be one of them). If they have a sense of entitlement, it's more than likely because their parents made them believe they should by providing them with the best money could buy without having to earn it.

These young co-workers are from your children's peer group who probably have some growing up to do but under no circumstance should you treat them like kids. They are in the same work space as you are for some of the same reasons. They have student loan and/or credit card debt, daily living bills to pay, and, perhaps, a mouth or two to feed. Some are also trying to get ahead—to establish a career to improve their financial wealth.

According to statistics released by The U.S. Census Bureau, *Young Adults, Then and Now*, these are some other facts about the Millennial Generation:

- More Millennials are living in poverty and fewer are employed, compared with Baby Boomers in 1980
- The share of young adults that are racial or ethnic minorities has doubled over the last 30 years
- 1 in 4 young adults speaks a language other than English at home
- Unlike prior generations of young adults, the majority of Millennials have never been married

- Young adults earn $2,000 less today in the work-place than young adults did in 1980

When it comes to education, more Millennials have a college degree than any other generation.

As a matter of fact, according to a national survey conducted by EY and the Economic Innovation Group (released September 2016), two-thirds of Millennials believe having a great education is important to getting ahead in life, but less than half (49 percent) believe that the benefits of a college education will be worth the cost. The survey also pointed out that 52 percent of Millennials will have taken on student loan debt and 43 percent believe that student debt has limited their career options. It's a well-known fact that "many Millennials entered the workforce in the midst of a deep economic crisis and today find themselves racked by student debt and lacking confidence in most American institutions."[4]

As for the work environment, a study found that 79 percent of Millennials think they should be allowed to wear jeans to work compared to only 6 percent of baby boomers. Further research indicates these young people are more apt to look for work with companies that have flexible schedules, a relaxed environment, and strong benefit plans that include health and wellness programs. Matt Schuyler, Chief Human Resources Officer for Hilton Worldwide said their new 10-week fully paid parental leave was driven by Millennials.

---

4   Source: National Survey on Millennials 9/22/2016 eig.org/millennial

That's because adults younger than 35 make up nearly half of Hilton's workforce and will soon be three-quarters. Schuyler also said, "The paid parental leave policy was instituted, in part, to be able to attract and retain the workforce of today and tomorrow." There's a direct connection between the investment in the health and wealth of employees and their level of engagement and productivity according to Donna Carbell, Senior Vice President of Group Benefits at Manulife.

More of these young employees also express a desire to become entrepreneurs rather than work for someone else—unlike many like baby boomers who chose to try to climb their way up the corporate ladder.

That's who we're dealing with.

"The greatest discovery of any generation is that a human being can alter his/her life by altering his/her attitude."

~William James

MILLENNIAL ATTITUDES TOWARD BABY BOOMERS

I don't think Millennials hate baby boomers but they can surely find a number of good reasons not to like us very much.

Some members of Gen Y could argue our generation was responsible for ruining the economy. Financial scandals involving baby boomer men like Kenneth Lay (Enron), Jeffrey Skilling (Enron) Bernie Madoff (Ponzi scheme), Ivan Boesky and his "Junk Bond King" partner in crime, Michael Milken, all played a role in ripping the hearts out of hard-working Americans who believed in the American dream and trusted these thieves to help them achieve it.

Then you have former baby boomer Presidents and an entire United States Congress who created, passed and even relaxed certain laws over the last 20-30 years that would be stifling to future generations. For example, young people may be familiar with the Teenage Mutant Ninja Turtles but they probably know little about the NINJA (**N**o **I**ncome, **N**o **J**ob or **A**ssets) loans created under the former Bill Clinton and George W. Bush administrations. These were low quality subprime mortgage loans where the borrower did not have to supply verification of income, job, and assets. This ultimately led to the financial and housing crisis in 2008.

As of this writing, the national debt is about $19,404,383,126,105.06. Many Millennials blame boomers for this. In his article, "Baby Boomers: Five Reasons They Are Our Worst Generation" Gene Marks wrote: *"One of the major reasons our national debt is so high is because 40 percent of our government's spending goes to some type of insurance: social insurance, retirement, health benefits, Medicare, Medicaid, etc. These systems are bankrupt. But they're needed to pay for the boomers' healthcare and pension plans. People that were born after 1965 are working hard to make sure that the boomer generation gets their retirement and disability paid for by the government. . . . They like their credit cards and government secured mortgages on overvalued properties. They enjoy their malls and their cars and their houses and as long as someone's willing to lend them the money to buy this stuff they don't seem to care much about how it will be one day paid. They still represent an enormous voting block and have no intention to have this lifestyle threatened. This is the real reason Washington can't create a long-term deficit reduction plan."*

So, What do Millennials Think About Boomers in the Workplace?

Based on a number of studies and surveys, the general consensus is we are resistant to change, lack creativity and the good old boy network reigns supreme in corporate America.

During my own random surveys, these were some of the opinions and comments about us:

- They move too slowly
- They act like know-it-alls
- They believe they're ALWAYS right
- They act as if they never did anything wrong
- They need to be receptive to new ideas
- They need to appreciate new ways of communicating
- Keep up to date with technology and realize how prevalent it is in their jobs
- Learn how to listen and understand where Millennials are coming from

One young lady I interviewed said she thought Baby Boomers didn't understand there's a new way of life. Many in her generation are not interested in going to work from 9 to 5. Instead, they prefer a flexible work schedule. They also have more of an entrepreneurial spirit and don't want to be confined like a chicken in a coup on the job. She also pointed out that the days of her Millennial girlfriends coming home from work and putting on a housewives apron are over.

Since returning to the job market I've had my own share of challenges in dealing with Millennials and as I learned from a young lady named Brianca, who's had her challenges dealing with us—especially ME:

"In the workplace, working with older people can be both fun and FRUSTRATING. They forget that they were once our age. As if sometimes everything the younger generation does irks them and that irks us. Some walk around and feel they are due the upmost respect when none is given. Irks my soul. Because they are older they feel certain rules don't apply to them. Some look at you crazy because of the way you dress, talk, walk etc. Also Mrs. Bev some older people don't realize that we're in a new age . . . although the old school ways are much better to me than today's time. Your generation just doesn't seem to realize that we are in the 2000s things have changed a lot!

On the other hand, sometimes older people in the workplace are a blessing because some are very knowledgeable. Some don't judge and fit right in with the millennial generation.

For example Mrs. Bev, when I first met you, you irked every nerve and vein in my body, but I grew to love you and I respect your knowledge and selflessness that you show. I've learned a lot from you, and you inspire me in many ways. Having older people in the work place can open our eyes to what's going on around us."

Enough said. #noshade

"The key elements in the art of working together are how to deal with change, how to deal with conflict, and how to reach our potential no matter how old we are. The needs of the team are best met when we meet the needs of individuals first."

~Max DePree

Do's and Don'ts for Baby Boomers in the Workplace

I am one of hundreds of thousands of baby boomers still in the job market and currently working side-by-side with people the same age as my 27-year-old daughter. Needless to say, it can be very challenging at times and I can't count the number of occasions when I've heard, read or seen things that leave me speechless—and trust me that's pretty hard to do.

At work, I'm known as Mrs. BAM or Mrs. Bev. Most of the young people address me that way which I see as a sign of their respectfulness. There are others who show little or no respect, which I believe is because they see me as irrelevant in their world—but as I tell my daughter all the time, you don't know who knows who and who can help get you where you want to go. Just because they see me in this low-paying, no opportunity for advancement position doesn't mean I don't have contacts and can't help someone advance to a higher level. Millennials need to learn that baby boomers can help them in many ways as it relates to their career ambitions and goals.

Eventually, we will be making our exit from the daily grind but, for the duration, we will have to find a way to co-exist peacefully and respectfully with our millennial counterparts. So how do we accomplish this?

Don't . . .

Treat them like children: The last thing your younger colleagues want to do is go to work and feel like they're working with mom, dad or a grandparent. Even if they don't behave with the level of maturity YOU think they ought to display, they should be still be respected and acknowledged for what they bring to the table. They were hired for a reason just like you. (Perhaps they will be your replacement.) Scolding them, talking down to them or even ignoring their presence says more about you than it does about them. Their resentment for you will only continue to grow and, soon, word will get around amongst their fellow millennial co-workers that you are a pain in the ass and God forbid, should you need help navigating something on the computer.

Be judgmental: Okay, let's face it. We're all judgmental of some things or some people but you are not sitting on a jury at work. Don't allow the way you think Millennials should behave or what you see them do that doesn't meet your standards in the workplace cloud your judgment of their potential.

Be condescending: How many times have you said, *"Back in my day . . ."*? Every generation has its flaws so it's unfair to taunt a mature superiority over your younger colleagues. You weren't perfect then. You didn't have all the answers and you surely aren't perfect now. One thing young people don't appreciate is older folks at work trying to tell them the way they *used* to do it was the right way and the only way. Times have changed and ideas have advanced.

Hang out with them: It's one thing to sit with them at lunch and engage in harmless chit-chat or even go out after work every now and then for a drink, but it's an entirely different ballgame if you are choosing to socialize with them at their favorite hang-out on the weekends and challenge them to beer chugging contests. You may be considered the "cool boomer" but not much respect will be attached to it especially if they happen to capture video of you passed out in a drunken stupor and post it on Snap Chat, YouTube or Instagram.

Do . . .

Be willing to learn something new: Simply put, this means being adaptable to change. Yes, we are used to the old adage, *If it ain't broke, don't fix it* but Millennials are of the opinion that you could be working with a broken or bad anything and not even know it so why not try another way to see if you can get a better result. Millennials are all about trying new ways of doing things in an effort to produce better results while baby boomers tend to get stuck in the habit of doing the same thing the same old way.

Embrace technology: Whether you like it or not, we live in the age of technology and, remember,

Millennials grew up with it. They understand its sig-
nificance and impact on daily work life and as I'm sure
you've witnessed, they can't seem to live without social
media. No, you don't have to connect with them on
Facebook or #hashtag them on Twitter but it doesn't
hurt to ask for help in navigating a complex computer
system you may be struggling with at work.

Be willing to help: *"College degrees and internships
have afforded Millennials the knowledge and newfound
skill sets to add to their portfolio, but inexperience and
greenness to the business world have left them with an
apparent lack of soft skills."* [5]

What we may lack in technology skills, we certainly
make up for in people/soft skills. We do know how
to communicate effectively face-to-face and that skill
has led to promotions or better paying jobs for us. We
have also learned how to develop transferable long-
term career goals, such as problem-solving, communication, negotiation and leadership.

We can certainly create value in a young co-worker's
career life by helping them develop in those areas. Of
course, they will be more receptive to your assistance
by the way you approach them. Dictating or mandat-
ing anything will get you ignored.

Show your wisdom: The beauty of aging is we become
wiser after learning from all the mistakes we made
during our younger years. (hopefully you have). No
need to demonstrate a *holier than thou* attitude but

5 Source: Millennials Need Soft Skills Training by Michelle
Eggleston

you can certainly be a shining example of what your Millennial co-workers can aspire to by sharing your knowledge and helpful resources. Let them know you were once where they are. Be open and honest with them about challenges they may face and extend a helping hand to help them achieve their goals if they have any.

Knowledge comes from learning. Wisdom comes from living. ~Anthony Douglas Williams

DISCRIMINATION AGAINST BOOMERS IN THE WORKPLACE

(my personal commentary)

Employment discrimination is not limited to race or gender. It is also based on age.

According to a researcher from the Center for Retirement Research at Boston College, potential employers are more likely to discriminate against older workers. Johanna Lahey sent out 4,000 resumes of people between the ages of 25 and 62 to firms in Boston, MA and St. Petersburg, FL. Her findings indicated younger workers were 40 percent more likely to be called back for an interview than an older worker, defined as 50 years and older. Furthermore, she cited the top 10 reasons why employers said OTHER employers might be reluctant to hire older adults:

- Shorter career potential
- Lack of energy
- Cost of health and life insurance and pensions
- Less flexible/adaptable
- Higher salary demands

- Health risks/absences
- Knowledge and skills obsolescence
- Block career path of younger workers
- Suspicion about competence
- Fear of discrimination lawsuit

Corporate America must take some of the responsibility for pitting the young against the old. Many companies don't want to pay for experience. They would rather hire someone with the ability to do the job for less money than to pay top dollar to a more experienced older employee. Some businesses aren't as interested in quality as they are in the bottom line: PROFIT.

The truth of the matter is baby boomers are living longer, healthier and productive lives and need to make ends meet just like their younger counterparts. Corporate America must be willing to recognize the pools of talented applicants no matter how old they are.

On a personal note, I know first-hand what it's like to be discriminated against in the job market. When I first attempted to re-enter the work force, I sent out hundreds of resumes for jobs in my field of expertise as well as menial jobs I felt I could do with my eyes closed (and one hand tied behind my back). I got very few responses and the ones I did get thanked me for applying but indicated the position had already been filled.

I'm sure I'm not the only one.

"I can do things you cannot, you can do things I cannot; together we can do GREAT THINGS."

~Mother Theresa

KEYS TO WORKING TOGETHER SUCCESSFULLY

Despite what the naysayers think, Baby Boomers and Millennials can work together and they can teach each other a thing or two in the process.

Appreciate Each Other's Strengths (and capitalize on them): Accept the fact that the Millennial(s) who works beside you has the clear advantage when it comes to technology. They grew up with broadband (do you even know what that it is?), smartphones, laptops, tablets and social media being the norm and, yes, they expect instant access to information. Most of them will be willing to share their knowledge if you ask.

We, as Boomers, have the gift of communication, writing, Company hierarchy, organizational skills and we understand the so-called office politics. We should not be intimidated or threatened by their presence. Instead we should be willing to share our knowledge and professional tips for their growth which could pay off in big dividends should they get promoted.

Be willing to accept change: *To fear change is to fear being challenged. To fear being challenged is to fear growth and new possibilities.* ~Former NFL Player Ty Howard

Learn How to Collaborate: When co-workers with different understandings based on their areas of expertise and level of maturity are able to share their knowledge, they are more likely to be encouraged to come up with new and better ways of doing things. It increases employee engagement. Furthermore, employees who feel as if they are being heard will be more likely to invest more time and energy into making a project work.[6]

Accept and learn how to give constructive criticism: Accepting criticism can be hard no matter who delivers it but if it's coming from your boss who happens to be younger than you, it can be especially difficult. It's almost like having your young adult child scold you inappropriate behavior. Ouch! Yes, it can sting. You might be tempted to take the defensive and argue your points as an explanation—but you'll soften the situation by being respectful and listening to what your young boss has to say. Also, it's important to maintain a positive attitude with a pleasant facial expression and body language that doesn't offend. Certainly, you have every right to voice your opinion about the constructive criticism but remember it's not always what you say but how you deliver it.

---

6 Source: https://fcw.com/articles/2012/12/07/collabora-tion-in-agency-environments.aspx

When it comes to giving constructive criticism to your younger colleagues, I am a firm believer that you deliver the message in the same way you would want it to be delivered to you. Yelling and cursing is never okay on the job. You may be angry over a stupid mistake they made but they are not your children and as I said in an earlier chapter they should never be treated like one. The way you deliver your constructive criticism may be the key that gets them on the right track and on the road to the success they seek.

Get to know each other: Okay—this doesn't mean you have to become bosom buddies or hang out on the weekends, but getting to know more about your co-worker(s) will help you understand them better. Learn about their interests and what drives them. You may find you share more in common than you think and when you understand them better you may be less reactionary when they say or do something that doesn't necessarily meet your standard of approval.

Who is Beverly Mahone

When I first moved to North Carolina from Florida I took a job where I was placed in a three-month accelerator program. The objective was to make me client-facing ready for my career goal of being a Financial Planner. It's not uncommon for this to be seen as your sink or swim moment.

The first day of real work I was greeted by Beverly Mahone. "Miss Bev" was instantly seen as the team mom who wanted to be a resource to anyone and everyone who asked. She had a knack for knowing how to motivate and inspire. She remembered everyone's names and birthdates and was always getting and having everyone sign birthday cards for fellow team members. She also sent out these daily inspirational messages, which I kept in a folder.

She reached out to me after hours in the office and at the gym—which is where we had some of our BEST conversations and really got to know each other. No one would have expected us to hit it off the way we did.

What impressed me about her was she had a successful career in broadcasting and developed a vast and diverse group of contacts. After reading her book, *How to Get on the News Without Committing Murder,* I knew she was pretty special.

Talking with "Miss Bev" forced me out of my comfort zone at times but that's where real dialogue began. I have learned and am still learning from her and, make no mistake about it, she remains a force to be reckoned with.

Respectfully submitted,
Chris Gure

Resources

What is a NINJA loan by Arnold Kling June 4, 2010

Millennials In The Workplace: They Don't Need Trophies But They Want Reinforcement by Jeff Fromm/Forbes 11/6/2015

USdebtclock.org

Usgovernmentdebt.us

http://www.phillymag.com/news/2013/12/13/baby-boomers-worst-generation/

Millennials Need Soft Skills Training by Michelle Eggleston http://www.trainingindustry.com/blog/blog-entries/millennials-need-soft-skills-training.aspx

15 Economic Facts About Millennials—The Council of Economic Advisors 2014

Daily Mail Newspaper (Greenspan comments)

https://onlinemba.unc.edu/blog/
geny-in-the-workplace/

http://www.elance-odesk.com/
millennial-majority-workforce

http://business.time.com/2012/03/29/millennials-vs-
baby-boomers-who-would-you-rather-hire/

eig.org/millennial

From Cooks to Accountants: Hilton Extends Paid Parental Leave To All by Jennifer Ludden Source: National Public Radio: All Things Considered 10/11/2016

Manulife ()

Kymberlee Holloway

Karkeshia Hart

Brianca Trent

Ellena Damarr (Gen X)

The Millennial Perspective

An old man said, "Erasers are made for those who make mistakes.

A young person replied, "Erasers are made for those who are willing to correct their mistakes!"

Attitude matters!

~www.dailyinspirationalquotes.com

PART II

Accepting the Baton from
Baby Boomers to Millennials

Changing of the Guard

You walk into your new-hire enrollment meeting to see a 50-year-old man fumbling with the computer and telling you to take a seat. It's a scene you've been conditioned to seeing throughout your academic career. The instructor introduces himself and tells you it will be six weeks before you actually start working, and he is going to be your guide to learning the "new computer systems". You instinctively roll your eyes and get your phone out. Without a tiniest effort you can find a YouTube video that will teach you everything this man knows about a "new computer system" in 30 minutes, not 6 weeks.

You take a deep breath as he hovers over the start button for the full display to come up as he moves over each option before landing on 'programs'. Think about how you wanted to start meditating as he accidentally clicks away onto the screen and is about to have to restart this 5 minute ordeal. What is this guy going to "teach" you next? How to open Microsoft paint? I've been ignoring my middle school teacher for years playing with that. Maybe he'll open your eyes to the world of Excel! You finished your capstone class in college with advanced pivot tables and if this guy pivots too hard he's going to break a hip.

Yes, a changing of the guard is taking place. With all of their fanfare and glory over the years, baby boomers are reluctantly realizing a new generation has arrived and we are setting the tone for the workplace of the future. We win, hands down, when it comes to technology; although, we may lose out on those soft skills like actually talking to each other face-to-face.

Baby boomers have been in the workplace and building relationships for years. They may have worked for a company longer than we've been alive. They are accustomed to making the high five- and six-figure incomes and used to running "the show" their way. You know what I'm talking about: "It's my way or the highway!" attitude.

But now, with more than ten thousand boomers turning 65 and becoming eligible for retirement annually, it's our turn to step up and take our rightful places in the workforce.

So, why is a guide like this necessary? It is important because as long as we enter and roam around the job market, we are more than likely going to be working side-by-side with baby boomers—and some of them are going to be our bosses. We are going to be challenged, daily, by the way they say and do things. We are going to be tested by their superiority complexes and their lack of desire to try something new, different, and creative. Some of them will even see us as a threat, intimidated by our very presence.

This guide is especially relevant if you are a Millennial trying to move up the corporate ladder, because you will need to know, and understand, what it takes to get there with the help of your baby boomer colleagues.

WHO ARE THE BABY BOOMERS?

The Baby Boomer Generation is made up of people who were born between 1946–1964. They are, more than likely, your parents or parents of your friends. If you're employed, there's some probably working with you.

To understand the vast differences between our generation and theirs, here are some facts:

- Color television was introduced to baby boomers in 1951, but it wasn't until 1971 that roughly 48 percent of American households had one in their living room.[7] Floor model TV brands, some with rabbit ear antennas, ruled the day. We, on the other hand, have known nothing other than color TV; and flat screens rule our day—the bigger the better!

- Protests against the Vietnam War were prevalent among young college students in the late 60s and early 70s. Those public demonstrations took a fatal turn on May 4, 1970 when four Kent State students in Ohio were gunned down by

---

7   Source: Color it color." Broadcasting. 26 Jul. 1971: 7

National Guardsman during a public demonstration on their campus.

- Along with the Vietnam War, boomers were also leading the charge during the Civil Rights Movement.
- They were also known for becoming the first generation to become openly infatuated with, and addicted to, illegal drugs. And the problem appears to be getting worse as they age. According to a 2012 National Survey on Drug Use and Health, it was estimated that the number of adults age 50 and older who will need alcohol or drug treatment will increase to 5.7 million by 2020—up from 2.8 million in 2002–2006. According to a study conducted by the Substance Abuse and Mental Health Services Administration, 75 percent of those surveyed reported that their primary substance abuse began before the age of 25.[8]

Adjectives they would probably use to describe themselves in the work place include: ambitious, competitive, loyal to company values and policies, driven, strong work ethic, effective communicators, etc. These same adjectives are what they think we, as Millennials, lack.

---

8   Source: luxury.rehabs.com/drug-addiction/baby-boomers

Young people don't know what old age is and old people forget what youth was.

~Irish Proverb

Millennials Meeting Boomers at Work

Make no mistake about it, when you walk into your first adult job, you are still the intern. Expectations from your supervisor might not be as high as you expect, but this leaves room to choose your own path. Flying under the radar may be your path of least resistance until you decide to make your next move.

Just like your parents, your job may be the place you spend the most amount of time in your adult life. You will probably come in contact with co-workers the same age as your mom and dad, and maybe some as old as your grandparents. While some of them will welcome you and seek your help, others may ignore you, or even give you a hard time (disrespect) as if you don't belong there.

As a millennial you are walking into a new adventure, while some of your co-workers have been walking this path for longer than you've been alive. This could be the peak of their corporate ladder and your coming in with new energy and a new perspective on how things should be can create some disdain from older colleagues. There's bound to be some resentment towards you if you're stepping into a role that took someone else 20+ years of work to get there.

Be understanding and know that these colleagues can be allies as easily as they can be enemies. You don't have to step over someone else who may be more than willing to help boost you up.

How Baby Boomers View Millennials

"Baby Boomers in the workforce are being replaced by young people who just don't match up," according to 90-year-old former Federal Reserve chairman Alan Greenspan. He believes the boomer generation is *"the most productive, highly skilled, educated part of our labor force."* He pretty much sums up the sentiments of many older adults who aren't convinced we can carry on the business savvy torch with a level equal to or above what they have already set.

So, what are some of the boomer attitudes towards the millennial generation?

Their Number One Complaint: We are Obsessed with Technology

Perhaps there is a lot of truth in that, but we grew up with it the same way they grew up with televisions causing some to turn into couch potatoes. Yes it's true, some of us can't live without our smart phones and snap chat, but this is a part of the new world we live in, and yes, we may post things on social media that our employers might cringe at, but on the flip side, if we love our jobs, we'll sing our employer's praises to our five thousand followers.

Millennials Have Earned the Reputation as the "Job-Hopping" Generation

According to a 2015 Majority Millennial Workforce study *(commissioned by Elance-oDesk and Millennial Branding)*, fifty-eight percent say they expect to leave their jobs in three years or less. In another survey conducted by MTV, half of millennials said they'd rather have no job than a job they hate, and 80 percent said our main objective in a job was one that "valued my creativity."

Some Believe We Crave Recognition

In a study from UNC's Kenan-Flagler Business School and the Young Entrepreneurs Council, 80 percent of millennials stated they want instant feedback and praise for jobs well done. The truth is we want to know when we're doing a good job and that we helped with the company's bottom line.

We Don't Take Criticism Well

If this is considered a negative, then it is because we were turned into the "participation trophy generation" as a result of all of those non-significant awards we won at the various sports and summer camps. The other point lies in how the criticism is delivered. I believe it's fair to say some baby boomers in managerial positions aren't the best when it comes to knowing how to effectively communicate with their subordinates. They can be very condescending and show little or no compassion.

Millennials Are Not Loyal to Their Employers

LOYAL is a strong word. It means you are totally committed; totally dedicated. This is how the Merriam-Webster dictionary defines loyalty: unswerving in allegiance: as *a:* faithful in allegiance to one's lawful sovereign or government *b:* faithful to a private person to whom fidelity is due c: faithful to a cause, ideal, custom, institution, or product.

It's not that millennials are not loyal. The real question should be: *How much of an investment are companies prepared to make in us?* We are the future. And, loyalty should be a two-way street. If we invest our time and energy into your business, why don't you reciprocate in a way that keeps us happy and committed?

To be old and wise, you must first have to be young and foolish.

~Author unknown

UNDERSTANDING BOOMERS IN THE WORKPLACE

The Millennial Generation stands in stark contrast to Baby Boomers when it comes to working. We don't agree on when to arrive, when to leave, how to get the job done—the list goes on and on. The 9 to 5 *lifestyle* boomers have been accustomed to all of their working lives is not something that our generation created but it is something that we are excited about defeating. Going to work and going home with work is a part of their routine. They live to work, while we work to love.

Our generation doesn't put any value in the traditional work week. If we feel most productive from 6–10 pm, then why not use that time to work? We just spent 4+ years at a University strategically lining up our class schedule to never have to wake up early. We make sure that our breaks coincide with our friends and many of us have entrepreneurial dreams. The idea of working 9 to 5 for someone else to make a comfortable living doesn't compare to the dream of working 24/7 for yourself in order to spend the rest of your life doing what you want. According to the Cisco® 2014

Connected World Technology Report, *"roughly two-thirds of Gen X, Gen Y, and HR professionals believe that an organization that has adopted a flexible, mobile, and remote work model has a competitive advantage over one that requires employees to be in the office from 9 a.m. to 5 p.m. every weekday."*

Another obvious difference between the two generations is the Dress for Success mentality baby boomers seem to be obsessed with. Business suits may have been the order of the day 20 years ago, but who says that attire will make you work any more effectively. It only makes you look nice, but we all probably know someone who dresses very well but doesn't have much to offer professionally. A study found that Millennials would like casual Fridays almost every day. Seventy-nine percent think they should be allowed to wear jeans to work, at least sometimes, compared to only 60 percent of boomers. An overwhelming 93 percent of Millennials say they want a job where they can be themselves at work, and that includes dressing in a way that makes them comfortable. Boomers, on the other hand, are more inclined to believe you need a standard professional look in the workplace.[9]

Millennials wholeheartedly agree with the Cisco Report. Maybe this is because our generation has a different outlook on the next chapters in life. We are not quick to get married—despite the new engagement you see every day on Facebook. Purchasing a home or car is becoming less of an accomplishment and

9   Source: Millennials vs. Baby Boomers: Who Would You Rather Hire by Dan Schawbel

more of a burden. These large financial obligations, that are much more common in previous generations, create the opportunity for us to be more nimble with career moves.

Baby Boomers see buying a home, purchasing a new car, and having a family as the *American Dream*. These are financial obligations to Millennials. The ideas of a 30-year mortgage, a five-year car payment, and children who cost $1,000,000 to raise from 0–18 years old don't allow for a gap in work history—and sometimes you just need to take a break from the rat race.

Our ethics and attitudes on how we go about our work-life may greatly differ, but we must keep in mind the fact that the job many of these Boomers are in now may be their last hurrah before retirement, so we can overlook some things they say and do. For example, if your boomer colleague wants to get into the office before the crack of dawn, so be it. That morning cup of coffee and newspaper before everyone gets there may be the only peace and quiet they have all day. Compare that to your meditation app.

They tend to be creatures of habit, so if you see them doing the same thing over-and-over again, and it works for them, don't try to correct them on a way you might do it—unless they ask, of course.

When they want to stay past normal business hours to work on a computer-driven project, remember they had to learn that updated computer network by reading the manual—not by playing with it for five minutes. You may be able to re-format all of your work to your tablet at home, but this is not as easy for someone who didn't grow up with the same technology that you and I did. Working in the office may be a badge of honor to a Boomer even though you see it as a ball and chain.

When it comes to communications, their style is not what Millennials are used to. Boomers would rather sit down and engage in face-to-face conversations while we believe we can communicate just as effectively in a text message and can abbreviate without using *correct* grammar. That 30-second text you just sent to 15 of your friends to let them know everything you've accomplished for the last four hours is probably not going to go over the same to your 60-year-old manager who has recently "mastered" emails, but still hits reply all at the worst times. If baby boomer supervisors and managers understood how much could get accomplished using texting as a resource, work productivity could go way up in a shorter amount of time.

When it comes to writing reports and/or making presentations, boomers definitely have the edge because they are communicators. In a survey of hiring managers, nearly 50 percent said Millennials lacked good writing skills, something boomers were forced to develop and typically do better. We can make an awesome, very graphic-detailed Powerpoint, but they are the ones who can interpret it to perfection.[10]

---

10 Source: https://www.bfscapital.com/blog/
small-business-hire-millennials-baby-boomers/

If you find yourself in a position of having to work with members of the baby boomer generation, my advice to you is help where you can, glean from their knowledge and experiences, and understand some of them are still stuck in old habits and routines that aren't easily broken.

Who is Chris Gure?

I met Chris in 2013, not long after I decided to end my entrepreneurial dreams and re-enter the job market. We ended up on the same employee team for a short period of time. From the first moment I met Chris I knew he was a go-getter and going places. He had that *look* that told me he had a vision and a plan and a goal. His attitude reminded me of this Les Brown quote:

"Wanting something is not enough. You must hunger for it. Your motivation must be absolutely compelling in order to overcome the obstacles that will invariably come your way." ~Les Brown

Now I have to admit, if I had never reached out to talk to him, I would've just thought of him as a preppy little white boy, born with a silver spoon in his mouth, and just working temporarily until he could get his hands on his inheritance. But the more we chatted, I came to realize Chris was extremely determined on carving out his own successful path in life and his parents just laid the groundwork (as I have tried to do with my own daughter).

What I like about Chris is he is very genuine and down-to-earth. His level of maturity for his age surpasses anyone else that I've met in his age group—although some of his funny Facebook and Instagram posts remind me how different our generations are. He can converse with you on just about any subject but his passion is financial planning. All you have to do is mention something about saving for retirement and Chris lights up like a Christmas tree—eager and willing to share his knowledge and expertise to help create and build your retirement portfolio.

When we had our first conversation about baby boomers versus millennials, I knew were going to hit it off and be connected in some way for a long time. (Plus the fact that our birthdays are a day apart.) We started bouncing around the idea of doing a project together to highlight the differences between the generations in the workplace and what Companies need to do to attract the best millennial talent, while maintaining a good, positive balance in the workplace with baby boomers.

Thus, the dynamic Baby Boomer /Millennial Duo was created.

Respectfully submitted,
Beverly Mahone

ADDITIONAL TITLES AVAILABLE

Whatever! A Baby Boomer's Journey Into Middle Age

Beverly's first book is an inspirational and humorous look at growing older through the eyes of the self-proclaimed baby boomer diva herself! Beverly keeps her story real as she addresses issues including weight gain, menopause, and middle-age dating. The pages are filled with stories that will make you laugh, cry, and shaking your head in agreement. This book got her featured in the New York Times Newspaper and on Fox News.

In her review, Renowned Poet and Author Nikki Giovanni said, *"I think your advice and your personal storytelling help bring out your religious beliefs as well as your love of people . . . . You are, I believe, the right story at the right time."*

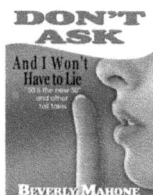

Don't Ask And I Won't Have to Lie

Don't Ask. And I Won't Have to Lie explores some of the subjects women lie about, why they do it and the role aging plays in the process. Once again, Beverly commands the reader's attention with her sassy sense of humor and keep it real style of writing.

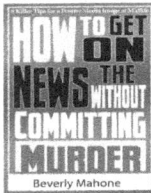

How to Get on the News Without Committing Murder

As a veteran journalist with more than 30 years of experience, Beverly offers 8 killer tips to help those seeking publicity on how to present a positive media image. This book serves as a guide for those who want to learn how to self-promote so the media will take an interest and want to feature them on the news, a talk show, or in a newspaper article. *How to Get on the News . . .* went to #1 on Amazon in June 2012.

CONTRIBUTING WRITER

Women of Color Devotional Bible

This unique devotional Bible was designed to encourage and strengthen women of color. Beverly was one of 52 contributors asked to participate. The devotional Bible is no longer available in print.

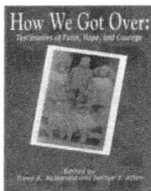

How We Got Over: Testimonies of Faith, Hope and Courage

Testimonies of Faith, Hope and Courage is about helping people to realize their fullest potential and enjoy an abundant life if they just stay focused on God.

(Available on Amazon.com)

WEBSITE:

www.beverlymahone.net

BLOGS:

www.boomerworld.blogspot.com
www.babyboomerbev.blogspot.com
www.businesswithbev.blogspot.com

www.ingramcontent.com/pod-product-compliance
Lightning Source LLC
Chambersburg PA
CBHW070911280326
41934CB00008B/1672